DATE DUE

What Living Things Need

Light

Vic Parker

Heinemann Library
Chicago, Illinois

© 2006 Heinemann Library
a division of Reed Elsevier Inc.
Chicago, Illinois

Customer Service 888-454-2279

Visit our website at www.heinemannraintree.com

Printed and bound in China by South China Printing Company Limited
Photo research by Ruth Blair and Andrea Sadler

10 09 08 07 06
10 9 8 7 6 5 4 3 2 1

Library of Congress Cataloging-in-Publication Data

Parker, Victoria.
   Light / Vic Parker.
       p. cm. -- (What living things need)
Includes bibliographical references and index.
ISBN 1-4034-7886-4 (library binding-hardcover : alk. paper) -- ISBN 1-4034-7892-9 (pbk. : alk. paper)
1. Light--Juvenile literature. 2. Photobiology--Juvenile literature. I. Title. II. Series.
   QC360.P386 2006
   535--dc22

                                        2005025129

Acknowledgments
The author and publishers are grateful to the following for permission to reproduce copyright material: Alamy pp. **5**, **6**, **7** (Tom Mareschal), **9** (Mike Stone), back cover (light bulb, Mike Stone); Bubbles (Loisjoy Thurstun) pp. **11**, **23** (torch); Corbis p. **4**; FLPA pp. **13** (B. Withers), **16** (Silvestris Fotoservice), **19** (Colin Marshall), **20** (Roger Hosking); Getty Images pp. **8** (Stone), **10**, **12** (Botanica), **14** (Taxi), **23** (shade, Stone), **23** (vitamin D, Taxi); NHPA pp. **17** (Daniel Heuclin), **18** (Ernie Janes), **22** (Andy Rouse), **23** (shadow, Andy Rouse), back cover (lizard, Daniel Heuclin); TopFoto pp. **15** (Bob Daemmrich, The Image Works), **21** (Gardner).

Cover photograph reproduced with permission of Alamy.

Many thanks to the teachers, library media specialists, reading instructors, and educational consultants who have helped develop the Read and Learn/Lee y aprende brand.

Disclaimer
All the Internet addresses (URLs) given in this book were valid at the time of going to press. However, due to the dynamic nature of the Internet, some addresses may have changed, or sites may have changed or ceased to exist since publication. While the author and publishers regret any inconvenience this may cause readers, no responsibility for any such changes can be accepted by either the author or the publishers. The paper used to print this book comes from sustainable resources.

Contents

Some words are shown in bold, **like this**. You can find them in the picture glossary on page 23.

What Is a Living Thing?

Living things are things that grow.

People, animals, and plants are living things.

Which things in this picture are living and which are not?

What Is Light?

Light is what stops things from being dark.

 Daylight comes from the Sun.

We also get light from lightbulbs
and candles.

Is Light Just Bright?

Light is hot as well as bright.

This is why it is warm in sunlight, but cool in the **shade**.

Candles and lightbulbs get hot when they are lit.

Be careful not to touch them!

Why Do We Need Light?

We need light to see things clearly.

Take this book and hide in bed.
Can you read the book in the dark?

Find a **flashlight** and try again.

Can you read the book now?

Is Light Just for Seeing Things?

We also need sunlight to keep us warm.

Our bodies need to be warm to stay alive.

12

Sunlight helps keep our bodies from getting too cold.

Does Light Keep Us Healthy?

We need a little bit of sunlight to keep us healthy.

Our bodies get **vitamin D** from sunlight. This helps us to grow.

Too much hot sunlight can make us feel sick.

It can even burn our skin.

Do Animals Need Light to See and Keep Warm?

Many animals need light to see. But bats come out when it is dark.

Bats have great hearing. They use it to find their way in the dark.

Many animals need light to
keep warm.

This lizard needs to lie in the sun
to warm itself up.

Do All Animals Live in Sunlight?

Many animals live in sunlight like we do.

But this mole lives under the ground in the dark.

Some animals live in the ocean.

The deeper they live in the ocean, the less light they get.

Do Plants Need Light?

All plants need light.

Plants mix light with air and water inside their leaves to make food.

20

Plants use this food to grow.

Can You Guess?

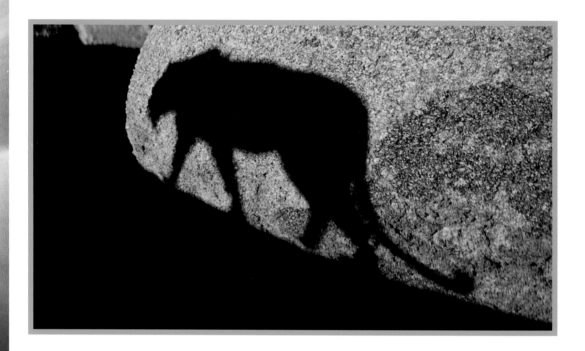

When you stand in sunlight, you make a dark patch. This is called a **shadow**.

Can you guess what is making this shadow? It is a big cat.

Glossary

 **vitamin D** something that our bodies need to grow strong. Our bodies get it from sunlight, and from foods such as fish, milk, butter, and eggs.

 **shade** an area out of sunlight, that is dark and cool

 **shadow** the dark shape made when an object blocks out light

 **flashlight** a type of lamp you can hold in your hand

Index

Note to Parents and Teachers

Reading nonfiction texts for information is an important part of a child's literacy development. Readers can be encouraged to ask simple questions and then use the text to find the answers. Most chapters in this book begin with a question. Read the questions together. Look at the pictures. Talk about what the answer might be. Then read the text to find out if your predictions were correct. To develop readers' enquiry skills, encourage them to think of other questions they might ask about the topic. Discuss where you could find the answers. Assist children in using the contents page, picture glossary and index to practise research skills and new vocabulary.